Original title:
Thorns of Thought

Copyright © 2025 Creative Arts Management OÜ
All rights reserved.

Author: Micah Sterling
ISBN HARDBACK: 978-1-80567-013-1
ISBN PAPERBACK: 978-1-80567-093-3

Fragments of a Fragile Dream

In the garden of my mind, I trip,
Over thoughts like hedgehogs, sharp and hip.
I laugh at clouds that dance and pout,
As they spill jellybeans all about.

Dreams flutter like butterflies in flight,
Tickling my nose, what a silly sight.
I chase them down with a giant spoon,
Hoping to catch one by the next full moon.

The Bramble's Embrace

In this wild patch of whimsy, I roam,
Looking for a quirky, sage-like gnome.
But every step, a poke or a pry,
I'm starting to think I should just fly.

With a giggle and a shuffle, I tease,
The pesky bushes swaying in the breeze.
They snag my shoelaces, what a scene!
A battle of wits with a leafy queen.

Stitches of Scrutiny

With a needle made of laughter, I sew,
The clumsy mishaps I seem to grow.
Each thread a story, pokes and jabs,
Turning my fumbles into funny jabs.

I quilt my thoughts like patchwork dreams,
Filling them with mismatched, silly seams.
An odd assembly, but oh so bright,
In the fabric of humor, I take flight.

The Thorny Garden of the Soul

In my soul's wild garden, I play,
With flowers that giggle and dance all day.
But watch your step! The ground is pranked,
With flowerpots that throw water, you're tanked!

The weeds whisper jokes, they tickle my mind,
As I untangle vines that twist and bind.
In this messy plot where laughter rules,
I grow my joy beyond the tools.

Thickets of Doubt

In the garden of my mind, weeds grow,
Funny thoughts dance, like a circus show.
A potted plant speaks, I start to giggle,
While pondering life, I begin to wiggle.

Should I plant a rose or a cactus green?
This garden of choices, a humorous scene.
Decisions are ticklish, and I can't decide,
So I'll let the daisies take me for a ride.

Roughness in Rapture

Romance is sweet, but oh, the scrapes,
My clumsy heart often takes funny shapes.
A hopeful glance turns into a stare,
While soap bubbles burst in the love-filled air.

Kisses like bees, buzzing here and there,
My darling's laughs make me tug at my hair.
In rapture we tumble, a comical fall,
With patches of laughter, we conquer it all.

The Painful Blossom

A flower blooms with a prickly face,
It giggles and wobbles, keeping its place.
Its petals uncoil with a sudden tease,
While I tiptoe gently, avoiding unease.

I reached out to touch, but it poked me back,
A painful giggle, a colorful crack.
In pain comes a laugh, in laughter I bleed,
Blooms of humor sprout from my heart's wild need.

Puzzles of the Heart

My heart's a jigsaw, pieces askew,
Searching for love in a slightly odd view.
Each corner a chuckle, each edge a grin,
Trying to fit in where giggles begin.

What's missing from this silly completion?
Is it laughter or love that fuels my ambition?
A riddle of joy, entwined in the fun,
In the puzzles of hearts, we forever run.

The Weeds of Hope

In the garden of my mind, they sprout,
Laughing loudly, no sign of doubt.
Petals made of paper, bright and bold,
Worries fly away, like tales untold.

Every thought a flower, wild and free,
Dancing in the wind, not a single plea.
The roots are tangled, quite a mess,
But oh, what joy in the chaos, I confess!

Sunshine spills like lemonade, sweet,
While bees gossip about my silly feat.
Each bloom a giggle, each stem a jest,
In this riot of greens, I feel so blessed.

So let them grow, my jolly weeds,
Water them with laughter, fulfill their needs.
No gardener's tools, only a grin,
As I tend to dreams that bubble within.

Cracks in the Facade

Behind the walls, there's a funny flair,
Laughter seeps through, fills the air.
Cracks carved by time and a joke or two,
What's breaking down is the serious view.

With every chip, a story flows,
Of pancake fails and pet nose blows.
The plaster's odd, a funny patch,
Cover-ups are really quite a catch.

Within the gaps, squirrels play charades,
While I sip tea, counting the parades.
Each flaw a chance for a chuckle or cheer,
In this silly fortress, I have no fear.

So smile at the fractures, don't walk past,
For behind every seam, joy's found at last.
The facade may crumble, but humor stays,
Cracking up, I'll laugh through the days.

Entangled Dreams

In a tangle of dreams, I took a dive,
Chasing unicorns and a bee that drives.
Daisies point to a snoozing cat,
While rainbows lead me to breakfast flat.

A web of wishes, sticky and bright,
Where jellybeans twinkle like stars at night.
Each thought's a noodle, slippy and weird,
As I trip through daydreams, slightly steered.

I ride on clouds made of whipped cream,
With a sidekick toaster, straight from a meme.
We giggle and wiggle as we float around,
In this jumbled rainbow, joy knows no bound.

So tie me up in this glorious mess,
Where dreams dance silly, I must confess.
Untangle the laughter, let it take flight,
In the land of nonsense, everything's right.

Echoing Whispers of Pain

Hush now, listen, what's that around?
It's the echoes of blunders, laughter unbound.
Whispers of mishaps, tickles that sting,
With every faux pas, more giggles take wing.

A slip on the dance floor, a trip on the rug,
The cat, too, joins in for a laugh and a shrug.
Voices of fumbles, in chorus they sing,
Turning blunders to jewels, they brightly cling.

From stumbles and tumbles to chocolate smears,
Each laugh a bandage for lingering fears.
Wrap me in humor, spin tales from despair,
For laughter's the remedy that's always there.

So join the symphony of sweetly absurd,
Where echoes of pain are simply unheard.
Let's tickle the shadows till they just fade,
In this merry cacophony, we've got it made.

The Beauty of Jagged Edges

In a garden of giggles, the prickles do sway,
Fashioned in fancy, they lead me astray.
I sit on a cushion, with laughter so loud,
Who knew my own brain was such a wild crowd?

With each quirky thought, a blade starts to dance,
Twirling and whirling, it gives me a chance.
To tickle my fancy and poke fun at my fears,
While I navigate life, avoiding those tears.

Seeds of Struggle

Planting my thoughts in a garden of jest,
Some sprout with delight, others fail the test.
I water with laughter, sunshine my best friend,
But a few became weeds, they won't meet their end.

Oh, the seeds I have sown, they're tangled and wild,
With some blooming brightly, and others quite riled.
Each thought that I nurture, a comical bloom,
As I laugh through the garden, lightening the gloom.

The Balance of Blades

In the tango of chaos, each edge has its say,
A slip on the dance floor, oh what a display!
With thoughts that are sharp, and some that are sweet,
I stumbled, I fumbled, but got back on my feet.

Like juggling knives with a wink and a grin,
The balance is tricky, yet I'm eager to win.
Each chuckle a bandage, I patch up the nicks,
As I whirl through the madness and dodge the sharp kicks.

Vexations in the Underbrush

Amidst leafy disturbances, thoughts rush out to play,
Unruly ideas that wiggle away.
I chase after giggles that tease and elude,
While laughter erupts from the ruckus I brood.

These playful distractions, they vie for a chance,
To whip up a whirlwind, to frantically dance.
Yet beneath all the chaos, a lesson I find,
Is laughter's the antidote for a vexed mind.

The Thorny Path of Insight

In the garden of my mind, I stroll,
Bumping into a prickly soul.
Each idea shuffles, it's true,
Wearing a pointy shoe!

Punctured Hopes

My dreams, like balloons, take to the air,
But sharp wit pops them with flair.
"Oh no, not again!" I pout,
As my plans float whimsically out!

Sheltered by Shadows

In the shade, my thoughts take a nap,
But sneaky quips spring the trap.
I chuckle at jokes that don't land,
Like confetti tossed by a clumsy hand!

The Bristle of Consciousness

Awake at dawn, my mind's a mess,
Ideas wander, nothing to press.
Each notion jabs with a friendly poke,
Leaving me gasping, stifling a joke!

The Harvest of Heavy Thoughts

In a garden where my mind does roam,
Thoughts grow wild, far from home.
Each one heavier than a stone,
I ponder and fret, all alone.

With smiles hiding amidst the weights,
I giggle at my own debates.
A crop of worries, ripe yet spry,
Can laughter be the reason why?

Choked by Thickets

I wandered through the woods of me,
Where thoughts like vines grow endlessly.
They twist and tangle, grab my shirt,
I laugh aloud, though it can hurt.

Each thought a branch, I dance around,
My feet get stuck, I'm trapped, I'm bound.
But oh, the joy in getting stuck,
For laughter's bloom can ship a truck!

The Unhappy Blooms

Petals of worries begin to wilt,
In my mind's garden, it's built.
They moan and groan, quite the sight,
Yet cause a chuckle, pure delight.

"Why so sad?" I tease the bowl,
"Pick a sunny spot, unroll your soul!"
With every pout, they tickle me,
These blooms of gloom, oh can't you see?

Riddles Wrapped in Briars

In a maze where secrets hide,
Riddles dance, come take a ride.
They prickle like a spiky thorn,
Yet make me laugh, I'm never worn.

Each twist a giggle, each turn a prank,
In the thicket, thoughts earn rank.
Wrapped in joy, they tease and jest,
A riddle's fun, it's quite the quest!

In the Garden of Dilemmas

In the garden where ideas play,
Butterflies dance, but go astray.
Petals whisper, secrets they keep,
Yet weeds of worry take quite a leap.

Laughter blooms in colors so bright,
But then rainclouds threaten the light.
A jester bee buzzes, full of glee,
As thoughts tie knots for all to see.

Sunflowers twist, pondering their height,
While daisies giggle, lost in delight.
The carrots debate beneath the ground,
With humor sprouting all around.

In this patch of worries and fun,
We harvest laughs 'til the day is done.
For in each mix-up, joy we find,
In the garden of thoughts, so unrefined.

Braided Tangles of Thought

In the tangle of ideas untamed,
A twist and a turn, none are ashamed.
Like spaghetti flung with delight,
Fettuccine fun in the moonlight.

Knotted arguments strut down the lane,
While giggling logic joins the refrain.
Every twist leads to giggling fate,
As chaos and reason start to relate.

A wise old owl winks from a tree,
"Embrace the mess! Join the spree!"
Colors collide, like paint in a jar,
Each swirl a punchline—Whoa! How bizarre!

Laughter echoes, thoughts intertwine,
A bouquet of ideas, oh so divine.
In the braid of our minds, humor persists,
In tangled thoughts, joy's always in the midst.

The Stretching Vines of Becoming

Vines that twist, reaching for the sky,
Each leaf a dream, a curious why.
Climbing along the fence of doubt,
With a chuckle, they figure it out.

Bouncing thoughts bounce from vine to vine,
A playful dance in zigzag line.
Grapes of laughter roll down the way,
Fruity puns brighten the gray.

The sun peeks through, casting a grin,
While squirrels debate if they should dive in.
"Growing is hard, but let's make it fun!"
They murmur and giggle, till day is done.

And so these vines, with their joyous sway,
Define the path in a silly way.
In each stretch and twist, something new we find,
In the garden of growth, the heart is aligned.

Friction of Flowering Ideas

In a field where thoughts start to bloom,
Ideas collide, and make quite a room.
Like bees at a buffet, buzzing around,
They bump and they jiggle, oh what a sound!

Every petal a pun, each stem a joke,
The daisies chuckle, together they poke.
In the bustle of blooms, the air is thick,
With fragrant laughter, the clock is a trick.

A rose says, "Why so prickly with glee?"
While the lilacs smile, "We already are free!"
Mixing and matching in joyous accord,
Even thorns laugh, keeping humor explored.

For in the ruckus of flowering minds,
Where friction ignites, no dullness finds.
So dance in the garden of whims, my friend,
Where laughter and bloom together transcend.

Riddles Wrapped in Barbs

Why do cats sit on my lap?
Maybe they're planning a cap!
A riddle disguised as a coat,
With barbs that cause hope to float.

Do I take this path or that?
My brain is under constant combat.
Each choice a prickly affair,
Wrapped tight in mischief's snare.

A joke like a cactus's sting,
Makes me laugh at everything.
Why do I wear mismatched shoes?
Oh, life loves planting odd clues.

Tickled by thoughts that misbehave,
I laugh at the wisdom I crave.
For every barbed question I face,
I find joy in this tangled embrace.

Painful Blossoms of Knowing

If I knew what I don't know,
I'd surely have a great show.
But wisdom pricks like sharp confetti,
With petals that poke but seem petty.

Why did the chicken cross the road?
To avoid a mental overload!
Each answer brings another twist,
Like a punchline we can't resist.

Learning's a garden of jumbled weeds,
Sprouting knowledge while the brain feeds.
But laughter's the cure for every poke,
For we bloom where the giggles choke.

Knowing can sting like a bee's flight,
Yet humor glows in the cold night.
With every thorn, a joke might sprout,
In the painful blossoms of doubt.

The Stubborn Roots of Dilemma

Why do I cling to my silly doubts?
Like roots that pull on my brain's shouts.
Each question's a stubborn little sprout,
Chasing answers that flitter about.

If I push, will I trip on my shoes?
The dilemma begins to amuse.
With roots tangled in laughter's tune,
I ponder the light of the moon.

Why pick between two lovely pies?
When both could bring joyous sighs.
Yet here I jiggle in each thought,
Wrestling with dilemmas I caught.

So I skip through this garden of choice,
Finding humor in each voice.
For the roots may be stuck deep in mirth,
But laughter's the fruit that gives birth.

Crushed Petals of Ambivalence

Here I stand on a wobbly fence,
Torn between two dreams, oh, what a tense!
With crushed petals under my feet,
Ambivalence gives my heart a beat.

Is this the best flavor of ice cream?
Or should I try the new, wild dream?
Every scoop like a puzzling jest,
In this creamy confusion, I jest.

Oh, sweet indecision's a dance, so grand,
With sprinkles of chaos at my hand.
I laugh at the choices I face,
In this whimsical, bittersweet chase.

For crushed petals bring giggles and cheer,
In the garden of thoughts, I steer.
Each moment, a chance to misplay,
In the game of ambivalence, hooray!

Unruly Roots of Reason

In the garden where my thoughts roam,
I tripped on ideas, they called me home.
A tangle of whims, with no clear path,
I laughed out loud, in reason's wrath.

The whimsies sprout like mushrooms wild,
A playful jester, a giggling child.
They twist and turn, make nonsense bright,
In the chaos, I find pure delight.

With every step, a new surprise,
A wobbly dance, beneath the skies.
I juggle dreams like clumsy clowns,
Who knew deep thoughts wore silly crowns?

So let them grow, those roots of mine,
In the garden of jest, where punchlines shine.
I'll weed the worries, sow some cheer,
For laughter blooms, when reason's here.

Rustling in the Overgrowth

Amid the leaves, my thoughts do hide,
With giggles stuck, like weeds inside.
They rustle softly, like leaves in spring,
Each whispering doubt wears a comical wing.

I wander paths where sanity sways,
In a merry dance, through foggy haze.
Those jumbled musings, vague and absurd,
Chase me around like a frightened bird.

Tangled ideas like vines entwine,
Each twist a riddle, oh how divine!
Laughter erupts from pathways obscure,
Finding joy in knots, strange and pure.

So I laugh with the rustle, adapt to the mess,
For the joy of confusion, I gladly confess.
In the overgrowth, where silliness thrives,
The wild thoughts dance; the heart surely dives.

Shadows of Anxiety

In the corners where worries play,
Shadows of thoughts come out to sway.
They prance around in ridiculous shoes,
As I chuckle softly, I've got nothing to lose.

Each fluttering fear, a puppet on strings,
They sway to the music my giggling heart sings.
With every quirk, I give them a spin,
Turning dread into laughs, oh let the fun begin!

A creature of panic, I'll humor with glee,
Dancing with shadows, come join me!
For every clumsiness, a chuckle shall rise,
Anxieties melt with laughter's surprise.

So here in the gloom, where silliness thrives,
Shadows become friends, as the laughter dives.
Through the jumbled fears, my spirit will float,
With giggles and jests, I'll merrily gloat.

Gentle Hurdles of the Heart

I face hurdles with a wink and a grin,
Those gentle giants, where fun begins.
Each little stumble, a jolly surprise,
In the game of love, my spirit flies.

The heart does somersaults, takes leaps of joy,
Over mounds of awkward, oh what a ploy!
With laughter in hand, I bound and weave,
In the dance of affection, who can grieve?

These gentle hurdles turn giggles to art,
As love's playful jinx gives me a start.
I tumble and tumble, a joyous parade,
Each misstep's a chance for new jokes to be made.

So I greet each hurdle with a silly cheer,
They're not obstacles, just moments to steer.
In the heart's vast playground, laughter will play,
Through gentle hurdles, I'll find my way.

Barbs of the Mind

Ideas bounce like rubber bands,
Twisting, turning, getting stuck.
Thoughts like squirrels, they scamper fast,
Suddenly pause—oh what the cluck!

Worries poke like sneaky pricks,
Tickling my brain in a silly way.
Laughing at the chaos of my mind,
Why do I even think today?

The plans I make, a tangled mess,
A comedy where I'm the star.
Each moment slips, a jester's jest,
And here I am, with my little jar.

So I'll embrace this wacky ride,
Invite the giggles, join the fray.
Mind's mischief, I'll take in stride,
For laughter's best at the end of the day.

Whispers in the Underbrush

In the thicket where thoughts do roam,
Critters chatter, oh what a show!
Conversations twist like vines around,
Jokes pop up—what a weird tableau!

Rustling leaves, the giggles sneak,
Mice recite a stand-up sketch.
Each whisper tickles the mind's peak,
What's the punchline? I'll fetch, I'll fetch!

A rabbit hops, with a jest so sly,
While chipmunks dance in a frenzy,
Sharing secrets, I'd like to try,
But instead, I just trip—oh, the irony!

So I'll frolic in this dark woods,
Where shadows tease, and laughter flows.
In the silliness, I feel the good,
As bright ideas sprout like flowers that glow.

Shadows of Introspection

Deep in the thought, where shadows loom,
Ghosts of choices begin their waltz.
They tickle my brain, start a mental boom,
As I ponder my fate in a bit of a pulse.

An echo laughs, what a raucous cheer,
They poke at my heart with a playful jab.
Cackles in corners, the thoughts appear,
And I can't help but join their fab.

Observing my life through a comical lens,
The blunders flash like neon signs.
Oh, how my spirit just whimsically bends,
As echoes of laughter blithely intertwine.

So here I stand, absorbing the jest,
In shadows where wisdom hides and plays.
Each misstep is just part of the quest,
To dance with humor in the silliest ways.

Jagged Edges of Memory

Memories crunch like chips in a bowl,
Some sweet, some salty, others go snap!
Reflecting on each dimpled stroll,
I chuckle at life's little mishap.

A puzzle with pieces that don't quite fit,
Reminds me of a game gone awry.
Here's a laugh, and there's a bit,
Of blunders that make me wonder why?

Each cringe recalls a silly faux pas,
Jokes ricochet off each jagged edge.
What's life without a laugh, ha ha!
I'll take the leap, I'll gladly pledge.

So as I slice through time's jigsaw game,
I'll carve out joy with each jagged piece.
For laughter's the flame that drives out the shame,
In the memoir of me, may the fun never cease.

The Unseen Bristle

In my mind, a prickly crew,
Waltzing wildly, just for you.
They gossip, twist, and poke around,
In every laugh, their hoot is found.

With every thought, a curious jest,
They tickle brains, and never rest.
One thought sneezes, another chuckles,
In panic, all my logic buckles.

Stroll down paths where figures frolic,
Spinning tales that are quite symbolic.
They jive and jiggle, hats askew,
A circus troupe, forever new.

So here's my mind, a merry maze,
With flares of fun, in all the haze.
Next time you think, don't be too meek,
Embrace the quirks, let laughter speak!

A Dancer in the Darkness

In shadows thick, a solo dance,
A jester prancing, given a chance.
Two left feet, they whirl and glide,
With thoughts like corks, they bounce with pride.

A flip, a twirl, a spin so grand,
The nightly musings take the stand.
A giggle here, a snicker there,
As brain-bubbles rise, floating in air.

With each misstep, a riot of glee,
Who knew my mind could twirl so free?
In darkness, light a candle bright,
To chase the fancies that delight.

As laughter echoes, shadows recede,
The dancer dips, finding the speed.
So join the fun, release your woes,
And see how wild the laughter grows!

The Netting of Nerves

Oh dear, what's caught in this grand net?
A tangle of thoughts, many upset.
Like cats in yarn, they twist and play,
Leaving sanity somewhere far away.

In every knot, a giggle hides,
We chuckle, flirt with happy tides.
Nerves are jangled, yet we can't stop,
The comedy show is quite the flop.

A clumsy thought, a fumbled rhyme,
Yet here we sit, enjoying crime.
As tangled nets become our guide,
Through laughter's door, we'll slip and slide.

So embrace the clumsy, the wild, the fun,
We'll laugh together until we run.
This tangled life, a jokester's dream,
Amidst the chaos, we'll always beam!

Underneath the Surface

Beneath this calm, a whirlpool spins,
With thoughts like fish that splash and swim.
A deep dive down, a giggle erupts,
From murky waters, chaos erupts.

A treasure chest of jokes and puns,
Where laughter bubbles, and joy just runs.
Fish flip-flop with tales to tell,
In this ocean, we all do swell.

So let's dive deep, let's take a chance,
To swim with giggles, to lead the dance.
An underwater ball, a watery spree,
Where whirling thoughts go wild and free.

Underneath, the surface gleams,
With silly dreams and giggly screams.
Join the splash, let's make a wave,
Through humor's depths, we'll always crave!

Fragments of Beauty and Sorrow

A smile can hide a frown,
Like ice cream in a gown.
We dance with two left feet,
While chocolate makes us cheat.

In laughter hides a tear,
Oh, how we hold them dear!
With cake crumbs in our hair,
We sing without a care.

Life's circus isn't neat,
We juggle beats with heat.
A clown with painted face,
Is still a warm embrace.

The Unseen Pricklers of Sentiment

Like a cactus in a dream,
Life can often make us scream.
A hug can feel so tight,
Yet leave us with a slight fright.

Why does joy look like a cat?
Purring softly 'til it spat.
The jokes we tell in rhyme,
Can sometimes feel like crime.

And though we make a mess,
Life's silliness, we confess.
With giggles in our hearts,
We find where fun all starts.

The Tangle of Awkward Realizations

Tripping on our words too fast,
Making moments seem a blast.
A wink that wasn't planned,
Turns awkward with a hand.

A dance step here and there,
We boogie with a flair.
Stumbling on a thought or two,
We laugh it off like it's new.

With mismatched socks we care,
Life's fashion faux pas flair.
Our quirks may steal the show,
As silly truths overflow.

Unyielding Pins of Perception

What's life without some spice?
Like sugar that feels nice.
A pinch of salt on cake,
Is a big mistake to make.

Yet wisdom's sharpest edge,
Can cut us like a hedge.
We meme about our woes,
As laughter overflows.

With each bizarre twist and turn,
There's much more left to learn.
So poke fun at the grind,
And leave the gloom behind.

Crushed Between Tension

Between the giggles, things get tight,
A dance of chaos, oh what a sight!
Laughter weaves through the tangled haze,
While reason plays in a dizzying maze.

A juggler's plight with pies in the air,
We tiptoe on dreams, but who's really there?
With every chuckle, a pressure builds,
Like soda bottles bursting, oh, what thrills!

Hats tipped down low, we stumble and roll,
In this circus arts, we play our role.
A twist and a turn, then slip on a shoe,
Bring on the laughter, it's all we can do!

When life throws us quips, we don our best grin,
For under the surface, the fun can begin.
So let's clink our glasses, toast with a cheer,
In the chaos of joy, we have little to fear.

Hardships Among Petals

A flower's bloom, a comedic sight,
With bees who juggle, oh what delight!
Petals all ruffled, they sway in the breeze,
While ants do a tango, and play as they please.

Among the blossoms, mischief ensues,
The butterflies gossip, sharing the news.
A ladybug slips on a droopy leaf,
Laughter erupts at her clumsy disbelief!

Sun shines on puddles where giggles reflect,
In this garden of fun, we garden neglect.
With every wink from the daisies so bright,
It's hard not to chuckle at nature's weird plight!

Through the thicket we wander, arms stretched in play,
Finding joy in the struggle, come what may.
So dance with a sprout, let the breezes flow,
In this whimsical chaos, let your laughter grow.

Strains of Serenity

In the quiet corners, jokes take their flight,
Where peace meets the punchline, oh, what a sight!
With meditative llamas in yoga postures,
Who knew tranquility came with such gestures?

Zen and a giggle, an odd little mix,
Sipping on sunshine, while balancing tricks.
A peaceful retreat can shift with a grin,
When laughter's the mantra, we invite the din!

As clouds play hide and seek with the sun,
Chasing shadows that dance, we frolic and run.
A ticklish breeze that offers a tease,
Serenity's laughter brings us to our knees!

So here's to the bliss amid hilarious strains,
Where chuckles and calm are both part of the gains.
Let's embrace the absurd in this calming spree,
In the silence of giggles, we all can be free.

The Silent Pull of Pain

A tug at the heartstrings, but sense the jest,
Like a clown on crutches, still doing his best.
With every fumble, there's humor to find,
In the orchestra of life, what's silly can bind.

The wobble of wisdom wrapped in a pun,
As we tiptoe through trials, still chasing the fun.
A toe stub here, a backflip there,
With laughter as balm, we shake off despair!

Through silent struggles, we wear our best smiles,
Turning groans into giggles that travel for miles.
In the circus of living where pain can reside,
We juggle our woes; we laugh at the ride!

So here's to the moments that make us all crack,
To the silent pulls that keep bringing us back.
Let's laugh through the chaos, unfold our delight,
For humor's the treasure that shines through the night.

Scratches of Insight

In a garden of wild delight,
I plucked a flower bright.
But ow, what a sting it gave!
My fingers, they misbehaved.

I thought I'd gather wisdom's cheer,
But ended with a painful sneer.
Each petal whispered secrets true,
Yet still, my hands got quite the blue.

With each bloom I want to share,
But fear the pokes that bring despair.
So here I dance amongst the pricks,
A jester's act with clever tricks.

Oh, Nature! Can't we play nice?
Your beauty comes with a hidden vice.
I'll wear gloves beneath the sun,
Lest I forget this prickly fun!

The Bitter Bloom

In a pot of mischief fair,
Grew a flower with a nasty flair.
Its petals soft, its roots a tease,
With every whiff, it aimed to please.

But oh, the tricks that it could throw,
A scent so sweet, but pain below.
I sniffed and laughed at my own game,
Now I bear the scratchy blame.

I tried to plant a tender seed,
But found instead a thorny breed.
Who knew joy came with a bite?
Next time, I'll wield a shield in spite.

So here I sit with petals bright,
A laugh in pain, a funny sight.
For every bloom, a lesson learned,
In jest is where my heart has turned!

Wounds of Understanding

Oh, the wisdom that I seek,
Comes wrapped in layers, oh so bleak.
I reached for truths with eager hands,
But all I found were prickly bands.

I wandered through the thoughts so grand,
Only to scare off my own hand.
Each insight teases so divine,
Yet snags my fingers, oh how they whine!

But laughter lives where pain should dwell,
As I recount my thorny spell.
With every poke, I find a jest,
Sure, this wisdom is a real test!

So raise a toast to understanding,
In every scratch, there's humor landing.
For through the woes, I see the fun,
In every wound, a story spun!

The Painful Sprout

Behold the sprout, so small yet bold,
With dreams of grandeur, or so I'm told.
But roots so sharp and leaves that stab,
Oh, little one, you're quite the brab!

I watered dreams and sang them sweet,
Yet found myself beneath its feet.
Each poke a tale of wild surprise,
Who knew growth came with such a guise?

But here I chuckle, what a sight,
This little sprout's a sneaky knight.
Plans for a garden, oh so bright,
Yet each new shoot brings comic plight.

So onward I trudge, with glee and pain,
In every bloom, a hint of disdain.
For laughter lives where pokes do sprout,
In life's great garden, there's no doubt!

Thickets of Hesitation

In a garden of choices, I stand quite still,
Where ideas poke me, giving a thrill.
Should I leap or just linger, in this green maze?
I ponder and chuckle, lost in a haze.

Every step feels like dancing on shards of glass,
Yet I can't help but giggle, as moments pass.
Decision's a pickle, a fruit gone quite wrong,
I hummed a small tune, forgot the whole song.

My thoughts are a jumble, like socks in a drawer,
I fetch one and trip over two on the floor.
Do I dive into wisdom or swim in a jest?
With options galore, I'm lost in my quest.

Pensive Prickles

Once I had a notion, sharp as a cake knife,
It danced in my mind, wanting a bit of life.
But it poked at my brain, like a cat with a toy,
I laughed at the gleam, 'tis a prickly joy.

Thoughts prickle my senses, a tickle of fun,
Like squeezing a lemon while chasing the sun.
In the garden of musings, I pluck at a whim,
And giggle at visions both silly and grim.

An idea sprouts out like a weed in the night,
I water it gently, hoping it's right.
It sneaks up to jab me, a mischievous leap,
While I snort and I chuckle, in laughter I steep.

Entangled Ideas and Shadows

In shadows of thought, where ideas collide,
A ballet of nonsense, come take a wild ride.
I twirl with my dreams, all tangled in glee,
Each notion a jester, come dance along with me.

They shimmy and shake, like leaves in a breeze,
Each idea I catch seems to giggle with ease.
Here's a wild story, with twists on the way,
As laughter pours forth, it just makes my day.

Yet some sneaky whispers creep into my scheme,
Poking and prodding at cracks in my beam.
In the whirl of creation, I find it quite grand,
While juggling these thoughts, I trip... oh! My hand!

The Cage of Silent Yearning

Locked in my noggin, ideas take flight,
They flutter and flutter, but stay out of sight.
In the cage of my mind, they rustle and play,
I giggle at wishing they'd just come out to sway.

I tickle the bars, whisper jokes that I know,
Of dreams that are ticklish, and thoughts that won't grow.

The silent ones chuckle, their humor is sly,
As I puzzle and grin, and let out a sigh.

With each poke of joy, I berate my own doubt,
Underneath all these wishes, my laughter bursts out.
So here's to the silence that's filled with sweet cheer,
In the cage of my dreaming, I dance without fear.

Hidden Layers of Emotion

Underneath my smile, I hide,
A pile of chaos, stacked with pride.
Juggling thoughts like butterfingers,
Suddenly, my sanity lingers.

Tickle my brain, what a ride,
In a circus of feelings, I confide.
Each giggle hides a deeper frown,
Like a clown who forgot his crown.

Spaghetti ideas all intertwined,
With meatballs of doubt, I'm less refined.
A smirk while tripping on my own shoes,
Laughing at life's peculiar blues.

With a wink to the mirror, I say,
"It's just another oddball day!"
Life's a joke, or so it seems,
Ping-ponging thoughts, bouncing dreams.

Temptations Among Thorns

A berry sweet thought entices me,
It whispers softly, "Just let it be."
But lurking beneath that juicy gleam,
Are prickly pangs that burst my dream.

I dance with my whims, what a tease,
Finding trouble like it's a breeze.
Frolicking around with reckless cheer,
And pricking fingers – oh dear, oh dear!

A candy-coated lie on a stick,
It tricks my mind, it plays the trick.
I dip and dive, then bump my head,
Pillow of petals, but thorns instead.

With laughter I stumble, careworn yet bold,
Each misstep a tale, each jest retold.
In the garden of wishes, I flip and flop,
Swirling in bubbles, never to stop!

Frustrations of Fragility

In a glassy world where whispers float,
I dance like a wobbly boat.
Planned a parade, but oh, what's this?
A splash of chaos turns bliss into mist.

Like a paper kite in a stormy sky,
Fragile dreams that flit and fly.
Each gust a giggle, each sway a sigh,
I fumble and tumble, oh me, oh my!

Tiny tasks with a giant twist,
I trip on to-do lists, I can't resist.
A comedy show in the theater of life,
Where clumsiness meets humor and strife.

Still, laughter bubbles through it all,
As I pick myself back up from the fall.
A fragile heart, boldly beats,
With every stumble, new joy repeats.

The Dance of Complications

In a ballroom of chaos, I take my chance,
With feet so clumsy, I wobbly prance.
Twisting thoughts in a tangled reel,
Missteps become the highlight meal.

Round and round, with a chuckle and spin,
I twirl with the problems that bubble within.
Each turn ignites a giggle or two,
As complications dance, I trip on cue.

"Oh dear," I say, "this isn't planned!"
Yet here comes the whirl, take my hand!
Life's a partner with mischief and fun,
Even when my best plans come undone.

So with a laugh, I'll lead the way,
Through the jumble and tangle of the day.
Our dance with woes, a merry blend,
Complications twirl, yet we pretend!

The Jagged Path of Understanding

I stroll along this bumpy way,
With potholes filled with thoughts at play.
Each step a giggle, each stumble a jest,
In this maze of musings, I'm never at rest.

A squirrel appears, wearing a grin,
Chasing my mind, but nobody wins.
We laugh at the chaos, this wobbly dance,
While shadows of reason twirl in a trance.

A map made of puzzles, a GPS lost,
Dodging the thickets, what a merry cost!
With every detour, I find humor's light,
Navigating nonsense, I'm ready to fight.

Yet here in this tangle, I find my delight,
Embracing the quirks that dance in the night.
A journey of laughter, oh what a truth,
On this jagged path of perpetual youth.

Invasive Thoughts and Their Lament

Woke up today with a thought that creeps,
Like a friendly raccoon that rummages deep.
It snuck in sly, with a chuckle and grin,
Now it tells me jokes that I can't let in.

These thoughts invade like a cheerful parade,
Each float a question, every word displayed.
With banners and trumpets, they shout and they play,
While I'm just here trying to make sense of the day.

A thought wraps around me, like vines on a tree,
Tickling my brain, oh what could it be?
I swat at distractions, they dance in my head,
But they giggle and dart, refusing to dread.

So here I sit, with a smile and a wink,
As ideas turn silly, and wisdom takes a drink.
In this carnival of chaos, I take my stance,
Embracing the madness, inviting the chance.

The Silent Scream of Tension

A tightrope walker in my own mind,
Balancing fears of all kinds.
I juggle my worries, a clumsy display,
Wobbling and bobbling, come what may.

Each thought pulls tight like a rubber band,
Twisting and turning, oh isn't it grand?
A silent scream caught in my throat,
While giggles abound, as sanity floats.

With every step, the pressure mounts high,
As laughter erupts, like popcorn, oh my!
Those giggly tensions that grip and embrace,
Become silly whispers in this wild race.

So I bounce on this line, a comedic act,
Laughing at worries, I'm wholly intact.
With silence so loud, and jest in the air,
I twirl in chaos, a debonair bear.

Scars Left by Whims of Introspection

I peek in the mirror, with a wink on my face,
Sparks of wisdom and folly interlace.
Each wrinkle a giggle, each scar tells a tale,
Of wild ponderings where reason did flail.

A poke and a prod in the depths of my soul,
Uncovering treasures, like a wayward mole.
The ponderings dance, like leaves in the breeze,
Tickling my senses, bringing me ease.

I muse on my quirks, with a chuckle so bright,
Those times I folded in the heat of the night.
The quirkiest marks from my journey so far,
A map of my laughter, my own shooting star.

So here's to the battles, the fun scars we earn,
Like badges of humor, for which we must yearn.
In the land of reflection, where jesters convene,
I wear every mark like a whimsical queen.

The Hidden Sting

In the garden where ideas bloom,
Watch out for the sneaky broom!
It sweeps away your grand intent,
Leaving behind just what's unsent.

A moment's thought can feel quite grand,
'Til it slaps you with a rubber band.
Your brain, it twists, your mind takes flight,
Only to crash without a fight.

What once was clear now turns to mush,
As you ponder, your thoughts do rush.
Like a cat that chases shadows fast,
You've lost the plot, but what a blast!

So tread lightly, dear friend, and wear a grin,
For the best ideas may come from within.
Just avoid the prickles along the way,
And keep the chuckles in full sway!

Tangles of Desire

A wish to have it all at once,
Can turn you into quite the dunce.
You dream of riches, fame, and cheer,
But find yourself lost in souvenir.

With every want, a twist and turn,
In the maze of yearning, you will learn.
What's shiny bright might rust away,
Leaving you with crumbs to play.

Beware the paths that lead astray,
For every choice, a price to pay.
Like a kite stuck in a tree,
Your dreams are fuzzy, can't you see?

So laugh a little at your plight,
Embrace the chaos, hold on tight!
In tangled webs of dreams we dance,
Sometimes a laugh is worth the chance!

Corrosive Curiosity

A question asked can lead to glee,
But beware the rabbit hole, you see!
What starts as fun can turn to dread,
When your thoughts begin to over-spread.

You seek the truth with eager eyes,
But stumble into jumbled lies.
Like a cat that finds a laser dot,
You chase the thoughts you soon forgot.

The more you pry, the more you find,
A web of madness, one of a kind.
As knowledge clings like sticky goo,
You're left with questions, not a clue.

So take a step back, and have a laugh,
At your own expense, it's quite the craft.
In quizzical journeys, there's joy to lend,
So ride the waves, my curious friend!

Fences of Wisdom

Behind each fence, a lesson waits,
But peek too close, and fate berates.
A wise old owl sits on a post,
Chortling softly at the foolish host.

We build our fences tall and wide,
To keep out doubts we cannot bide.
But as we guard each precious thought,
We find the fears we never fought.

With every bar, a riddle grows,
In tangled talks and mismatched prose.
What felt so bright can dim so fast,
You learn your wisdom's built to last.

So laugh with glee at what you've learned,
For every fence means bridges burned.
In the field of thought, just take your time,
And find the humor in the climb!

Prickles of Reflection

In the garden where ideas play,
A cactus shows up to join the fray.
With dreams so pointy, and giggles that poke,
Who knew deep thoughts could make us choke?

Sipping tea with a pensive frown,
A snail zipped by, wearing a crown.
"Life's too short for a slow parade,"
He laughed, as he left a humorous braid.

A bee buzzed in with opinions grand,
"Too many thoughts will just leave you tanned!"
They tickled my mind, these buzzing all day,
Like sprinkles of joy in a thought buffet!

Among those prickers that made us laugh,
A porcupine came with charts on his path.
"Let's plot our fun on a thorny sheet!"
He danced 'round the room, and we all missed our seat.

Barbs of Contemplation

Sitting quietly, my brain took flight,
A hedgehog stumbled into the light.
"Why worry so much over silly dreams?"
He chuckled at thoughts bursting at seams.

A cactus remarked with a pointed grin,
"Too much pondering makes the head spin!"
With barbed comments that brought forth delight,
We erupted in fits both day and night.

In the garden of giggles, thoughts took the stage,
Where nonsense was wise and laughter a sage.
With each prickly pun, we found our way,
And danced through the echoes of thoughts gone astray.

So raise a glass, with bubbly cheer,
To all the wacky thoughts that draw near!
For every barb that makes us cringe,
Is a tickle of laughter at every fringe!

Jagged Whispers in the Mind

In the forest of musings, whispers arise,
With branches and twigs that don funny ties.
Each jagged thought, like a boisterous prank,
Turning somber reflections to giggles, I thank!

The owls in their glasses winked with delight,
"Thoughts can surprise when they take flight!"
A squirrel in a hat, with a grin so wide,
Started a rumor he could not abide.

A bear chuffed in, saying, "Who needs a plan?"
"Just dance on your thoughts with a highly fine tan!"
Jagged whispers turned into a song,
Laughing it out, where we all belong.

So let your mind twist and turn, never shy,
For awkward reflections can reach for the sky!
In the weirdness, we find a quirky delight,
With jagged whispers that shine endlessly bright!

The Sharp Edges of Memory

Memories prance on a tightrope so fine,
With sharp little edges that sparkle and shine.
A giraffe with a bowtie recalls a good jest,
While a parrot squawks, insisting he's best!

A dance of remembrance, a slide on the way,
Where laughter incites all the clouds to play.
Each moment a poke that tickles the heart,
As mischief and joy create curious art.

Through wild tales wrapped in spiky delight,
We gather the giggles to share late at night.
"Oh, remember that time…" a friend starts to say,
And laughter erupts as we all save the day!

With sharp edges twinkling, we weave our own tale,
Of quirky adventures where fun will prevail.
So raise up your toast, to what makes us grin,
The sharp edges of memories always draw us in!

Brambles of Unraveled Dreams

In fields where wild ideas bloom,
The weeds of worry start to loom.
I tripped on hopes, a comic plight,
Then laughed at clouds blocking my light.

With every scheme that missed the mark,
I danced with shadows, quite a lark.
I'd juggle plans, they'd fly away,
Like kite strings tangled in the fray.

Each twist and turn, a merry chase,
A game of hide and seek in space.
Yet still I grin, with arms akimbo,
As wishes scatter, bright like a rainbow.

And though the paths are filled with spines,
I'll wear my jester's cap, it shines.
For in the mess, a jest I find,
Unraveled dreams, still sweet and kind.

Echoes of Doubt's Grasp

Hear that giggle, is it me?
Or echoes mocking my decree?
Each thought a prankster, sly and neat,
With doubts that dance on nimble feet.

In every corner of my mind,
The whispers join, a jolly kind.
They toss me jests, they poke and prod,
In every chuckle, a little nod.

I try to focus, pull it tight,
But laughter sweeps me from the sight.
Like kittens chasing after yarn,
My worries fade, they can't do harm.

With doubts that play a game of tag,
I'm left to smile, let out a brag.
In the labyrinth of whirly thoughts,
There's joy to find in silly knots.

Slicing Through the Fog

The clouds roll in, a foggy spree,
I brandish thoughts like swords at sea.
With each slice through the murky gray,
I'm searching for the sun's bright ray.

But oops, I tripped on a gust of sense,
My head now spinning, quite the tense.
Yet every wobble, every spin,
Gives rise to giggles from within.

In muddled haze, I skate along,
A clumsy dance to a boppy song.
With every cut, I change my fate,
And laugh at how I hesitate.

So here's to fog, the tricky mate,
With every stumble, I celebrate.
For slicing through the thoughts that swarm,
Can turn the chilly into warm!

When Ideas Turn Sharp

Some days my thoughts are dulled and slow,
Like butter gone and turned to dough.
But other times they glimmer bright,
And cut right through like pizza knife!

I ponder jokes, they seem so grand,
Yet loop-de-loop, they don't go planned.
Each pun I wield can sometimes sting,
Like bees that buzz around the bling.

But laughter leads me back to play,
As sharp ideas go whirr and sway.
I'll catch the dreams, see where they dart,
And wear the jests like artful art.

When wit gets sharp and thoughts collide,
I two-step through the laughter tide.
So here's to edges, jokes, and jives,
In the tangle, craziness thrives!

Anxious Echoes

In the mind's wild maze, I roam,
Thoughts like squirrels, seeking a home.
They chatter and dance, a raucous tune,
While I just wish for a nap by noon.

Questions like rubber balls, they bounce,
Worry's a juggler that likes to pounce.
Is it a bird? A plane? Oh wait,
Just my anxiety, feeling great!

I'm plotting escape, a grand old plan,
To run away, but where? I can't be a fan.
Every echo teases my troubled spree,
"Just have some fun," they mockingly plea.

So here I stay, in comedic fright,
Lost in the jests of my own silly night.
Laughter may scatter this mental mess,
But it's hard to giggle when thoughts are a stress!

Born from Prickles

In my garden of thoughts, a strange plant grows,
Its leaves poke out while I ponder woes.
Why do my ideas have such sharp ends?
As if they plotted to turn into trends!

Shuffling through plans that never align,
Each step forward, my thoughts intertwine.
It's like a dance with a cactus in hand,
Each twist and turn, not exactly what I'd planned.

Sorting through visions, I slip and I slide,
These prickly thoughts, I can't let them hide.
Yet, strangely they laugh, a party of one,
Who knew that confusion could also be fun?

So here's to the weeds that grow in my head,
With a tickle and itch, they dance in my bed.
Though they poke and they prod, I find them quite grand,
For every odd thought, creates a new strand.

Briars of Awareness

Awareness is funny, like trying to see,
Through the brambles that laugh just at me.
These prickers of wisdom poke at my ear,
Whispering truths I don't want to hear.

With every bright thought, a hiccup appears,
It's like juggling jelly while choking on fears.
I squint through the sharpness, searching for light,
But it's hard to be wise when you've lost all sight.

These points of insight are prickly and bold,
Like hugs from your grandma, both loving and cold.
Do I laugh or cry? The choice is so tough,
Beneath all these branches, I can't get enough!

So I tiptoe through brambles, a dance with a grin,
Trying to smile at the mess I'm in.
For even in chaos, I find a strange way,
To twirl through the worries and joke every day!

Frayed Threads of Clarity

In my quest for gold, I found a skein,
Of confused threads that chuckle in vain.
They knot and they tangle, a colorful mess,
Like my brain trying hard to impress!

Patterns emerge that lead into space,
Yet twist like a pretzel, full of misplaced grace.
Pull one loose thread and a thousand spring free,
"Oh look!" they giggle, "Come chaos with me!"

I weave and I stitch, seeking reason in rips,
But laughter keeps threading through all of my quips.
Life's a patchwork of giggles and tears,
Each frayed end closer to joys, not fears.

So I gather my strings, both tattered and bright,
Enjoying the journey, embracing the light.
For clarity comes like a joke in disguise,
When we learn to find fun in each twist and surprise!

Vines of Contemplation

In the garden where ideas grow,
A vine decided to take it slow.
It wrapped around my head so tight,
I wondered if it'd give me flight.

A bumblebee buzzed, quite unclear,
It asked my thoughts, 'Are you sincere?'
I chuckled back, 'Oh, what a tease!'
'Just trying to avoid some mental sneeze!'

Twisted Paths of Reason

I walked a path of logic's maze,
Where squirrels debated night and days.
They argued points like seasoned pros,
While I just laughed at their little woes.

The trees were nodding, wise yet sly,
As I strolled by with a puzzled eye.
The path twisted and turned all around,
Like my thoughts when snacks abound!

Petals Beneath the Pain

On a flower, I sat with a sigh,
Wondering if daisies ever cry.
A petal dropped, but what a sight,
It landed on my snack—what a fright!

'Is this a garnish or a prank?'
I asked the flower, my brain went blank.
It laughed and danced in the bright sun,
Said, 'Oh darling, life's just for fun!'

Echoes of Dissonance

In the hall of echoes, thoughts collide,
Where nonsense whispers, wild and wide.
A parrot squawked the latest trend,
As I just shook my head, 'Oh friend!'

The walls laughed back, with chuckles loud,
At my serious face, looking quite cowed.
Sometimes the noise just takes its toll,
And makes you wonder—Am I whole?

A Garden of Bursting Ideas

In the garden where mishaps grow,
Ideas dance like a circus show.
One's a flower with googly eyes,
Another's wearing a clown's disguise.

Here comes a plant that tells a joke,
But watch out for the laughter choke!
Bumbling bees buzz with delight,
Twirling petals in a silly fight.

Even the weeds have something to say,
They chuckle while getting in the way.
With roots that tangle and twirl about,
They laugh as they twist and shout!

In this garden of quirks and fun,
Every shy bud wants to run.
So come on and join the silly spree,
Where thoughts bloom with glee, wild and free.

Unraveled Threads of Perception

In a tapestry of thoughts so bright,
Threads unravel with giggles of light.
One loop pulls tight, then shoots away,
Leaving patterns that beg us to play.

A stitch tries to dance but trips on a seam,
"Oh no!" it squeals, "Was this in the dream?"
Colors clash in a riotous spin,
Poking fun wherever they've been.

The needle chuckles, sharp and sly,
While buttons roll off, saying goodbye.
Each twist and turn ignites a laugh,
Here's a quilt that's a total gaff!

But oh sweet unthreaded, merry delight,
Each snip leads to a fanciful flight.
With each colorful tangle and twist,
Perceptions ripple like an airy mist.

The Bramble's Path

On a path of prickles where giggles abide,
The bramble leads us on a wild ride.
Bouncing hedgehogs join in the cheer,
While snickering bushes whisper, "Come here!"

One bramble claims it's a royal crown,
While toads croak jokes that spin you around.
Each twist and turn tells a tale so bright,
As roses blush in the morning light.

Look out for vines that twirl and tease,
Hoping to trip with a giggling breeze.
But don't be alarmed by the playful dance,
Just laugh and sway in this silly prance!

The bramble's path is a raucous delight,
Each thorny touch tickles with might.
So skip along, let your worries fade,
In this wild garden that jests and played.

Softly Stinging Truths

Here in the garden of truths so mild,
Soft whispers tease with laughter wild.
A truth sits grinning with cheeky flair,
"Life's better when you don't really care!"

Bumblebees hum a sweet song of bright,
While honesty playfully takes flight.
With each gentle poke, they ring the bell,
Truths bloom like flowers—can you tell?

Come tickle a truth with a feathered jest,
You'll find that laughter is simply the best.
In a patch of giggles where insights roam,
Each insight here might just feel like home.

So tread softly on these petals of glee,
For truths may sting, but they're fun, you'll see!
With every soft poke, a smile will sprout,
Inviting all to dance about.

Grits of Turmoil and Reflection

In the pot of my brain, ideas stew,
Sometimes they bubble up, what to do?
I add a pinch of salt, a dash of flair,
But often they come out with a little hair.

I stir and I poke, in my mental mix,
Thoughts all jumbled, like puzzle tricks.
Whisking the chaos, I giggle and grin,
Craft a masterpiece, or just a din.

Yet amidst the mess, humor breaks free,
Finding the punchline, oh joy for me!
The serious gets silly, as I laugh aloud,
This grits of my mind, my own little crowd.

So here's to the chaos, the chuckles in life,
Mixing up thoughts with a sprinkle of strife.
In the pot of reflection, I play my part,
Finding joy in the grit, a laugh at the heart.

The Veiled Scepters of the Mind

Cloaked in whispers, thoughts creep and crawl,
Like sneaky ninjas, they dart through the hall.
With scepters of wisdom, they reign supreme,
But often, it seems, they just like to dream.

In regal attire, my thoughts take a seat,
Declaring their plans, but it's all just a feat.
They wave little flags, of nonsense and jest,
Ruling my brain with a playful zest.

Yet under their throne, I find a delight,
A jester below, turning gloom into light.
With every mishap, the laughter awakes,
As the veiled scepters just set off the brakes.

So don't take it serious, my royal decree,
For in the grand scheme, it's just a big spree.
Join me in revel, as thoughts come alive,
In this kingdom of humor, we all shall thrive.

Prickles of Perception

Perceptions are pricks, it's quite the affair,
They tickle my brain with a mischievous flair.
Like roses in gardens, too lovely to touch,
They poke at my senses, oh why do they clutch?

I tiptoe around, just trying to see,
The world through my thoughts, so wild and free.
But every sharp notion, like bees in a hive,
Buzz and they sting, oh how do I survive?

Yet nestled in thorns, a sweet nectar hides,
Inviting my heart where the humor resides.
I chuckle at pricks, this dance I adore,
With every sharp poke, I just laugh even more.

So bring on the prickles, I shall take a chance,
In this playful waltz, I'll gladly dance.
With laughter as armor, I'll bravely explore,
The prickles of fun, that I can't ignore.

The Grit of Reflection

In the mirror of thought, reflections collide,
Witty whispers and giggles, they jump and they slide.
With grit in my gaze, I laugh at the show,
As the serious moments are tossed to and fro.

I ponder the odd, the funny, the slight,
Nonsense that dances in daydreams at night.
With a chuckle and wink, I savor the glow,
Of reflections that sparkle, in fun they bestow.

So gather your thoughts, with humor as guide,
A journey of grit where laughter won't hide.
With smiles as my compass, I wander the scene,
Finding joy in the grit, in spaces between.

So here's to reflections, both silly and bright,
For every deep thought, there's a giggle in flight.
Embrace all the quirks, let the fun be your map,
In the grit of reflection, take a joyful nap.

www.ingramcontent.com/pod-product-compliance
Lightning Source LLC
Chambersburg PA
CBHW051647160426
43209CB00004B/817